Julia Budenz

FROM THE GARDENS OF
Flora Baum

WESLEYAN UNIVERSITY PRESS

Middletown, Connecticut

To my parents and sisters

"The Fire Escape" originally appeared in *Studia Mystica,* Winter 1980, and "Helicon," part 5 of "The Sheen," in *The Kenyon Review,* Spring 1983.

All inquiries and permissions requests should be addressed to the Publisher, Wesleyan University Press, 110 Mt. Vernon Street, Middletown, Connecticut 06457

Distributed by Harper & Row Publishers, Keystone Industrial Park, Scranton, Pennsylvania 18512

LIBRARY OF CONGRESS CATALOGING IN PUBLICATION DATA
Budenz, Julia.
  From the gardens of Flora Baum.
  (Wesleyan new poets)
  I. Title. II. Series.
PS3552.U3475F7 1984   811'.54   83-27409
ISBN 0-8195-2115-9 (alk. paper)
ISBN 0-8195-1116-1 (pbk. : alk. paper)

Manufactured in the United States of America

First Edition
Wesleyan New Poets

CONTENTS

FROM THE GARDENS OF
Flora Baum

The Fire Escape

1. Sky

It is propitious
When the clusters of samaras match the bricks
And gusts in the dry clusters
Match the flaps of the pigeons
And a white slant across the black slats
Mirrors the darks of the dapples of backs
And the straight metalled edge of the tall red horizon adjacent
Meets blue deepening.

Can I cut a temple in the sky
And see the eagles pass auspiciously?

Blue, cloudless, that was the first way she remembered it.
It was the first thing she remembered.
You could rest in it wherever you moved—
Manhattan, Brooklyn, Chicago, Delphi.
Was it the same in Delphi?

When the epigones piled up the columns again
A particular verticality reappeared—
That of man, the erect, the geometer,
The astronaut. Far above the cliffs
Eagles sailed among the stars.

In the city, locus of the marks of man—
The straight border, the measured line,
The parallel, the perpendicular, the plumb—
In the city, sky was indicated.
There might not be much of it, but you looked up,
Pretending not to so you wouldn't be noticed—
Above all you wanted not to be noticed—
You pretended to look down so you wouldn't be noticed—
But you looked up. At the end
Of the measured lines lay the sky.

There was that blue one over the red brick building,
On top of the even, counted rectangles.
That one you could sit and watch.
The old red blanket had been spread out on the slats.

Here, remember, there was no earth.
There was no air.
Below, at times, illegally released
From fire hydrants, water ran red.
The aether was the elemental thing,
Blue fire.

Intensest melody,
Voice from the doorway of being,
Hyacinth of existence,
Essence of forget-me-not,
Penetrant into the self's
Cerulean penetralia,
Throbbing with the sapphire
Throbbing of reflective self
Straight out to the edges of quest and question,

O be forever blue, unending patch.
But by then the steady flash was broken,
The azure species flattened.
It was not clouds, night, a closing of lids;
That fleeing of the gleam from behind wide-open eyes,
That was it. The morning-glory curls.
The squill in the brick-red pot has faded.
The bars grow cold against the bones of your back.

2. Tree

She saw the single, multitudinous elm.

The trunk with its primary branches
Is firm, is still. A motion inheres
In that stillness: all the growing, the upholding,
The struggle recorded in a stance—
Antaeus kept from the earth,
The discus almost hurled,
A slain god just arisen.

The moving branchlets with their moving
Leaves are at rest, are not uneasy,
Are at ease, are resting as unresisting,
As swans rest on the stirring stream,
As eagles rest on the warm drafts of late morning.

Here is a solitary being, self-contained
And self-directed; here two hug and kiss;
Here is the generous outreach, proffering
Of gifts; then follow revel, bacchanal
Of lifted arms, green brands alight,
Frisson of verdure; ladies come
With fans and trailing gowns.

A form, a formulation, an assertion
Builds as clauses rise and phrases dangle
Into a green flutter of interjections
Among which cluster golden promises,
Promising the post-autumnal blank.

Buds supply the wintry punctuation.

3. Season

Of significant instants in the shifting of the sun
That of September is felt the least.
One point in December holds a community's jubilation:
From now the days will be getting longer.
One March moment is a general celebration:
Now the days are getting longer.
June's peak is a public joy:
Now we see the longest day.
People petal streets and parks and beaches.
Eternal splendor gilds the common sun.
September twenty-third slipped by
With a cool exhalation across a red leaf.
She put on her plaid skirt. At supper
The windows were down,
The shades were down,
The lamp was on,
The book was open.
Life was private.

4. Temple

September becomes a place,
September becomes a temple,
And an hour of September is a cella in that temple,
A cell in which the monk walks up and down.
Walking is a moving of the eyes
In one place in one vision. Tears
Are not forming. Pears
Hang as dropped from their blossoms.
Full, the fern-leaf beech, with sky at its brim,
Uplifts, keeps on uplifting.
Uplifted, fresh as of spring, slender and green,
The pagoda tree's fruits and leaves, with sky between,
Rest in ecstatic levitation.
All is green and glitter, all is light and light,
Beneath the benevolent blue.

You find no long liturgy here,
No choirs, no stanzaed songs,
But brief petitions, terse monitions,
Eleison exclaimed, short sounds
Of blue- or red-vested priests on their rounds.

Then a quiet.

What is that behind me?
Who is that walking behind me?
Those are the first footsteps
Of the first fallen leaves.

Would these panes always stand
Between her and the world?
She wept. She was only seven.
The high fine lines were apocalyptic.
The tallest building in the world
Had darkly stood before her eyes.
She could bear to see through glass.

In the large room of November —
A hall for a Hrothgar —
The posts and beams were bared,
Some flames still flickered in the barberry hearths,
The golds and greens and coppers gleamed
In the tapestry of the beech.
Of the dancing, nothing remained
But the gray whack of her heels on the sidewalk,
The brown crackling under her soles,
The skirl and drone of leafblowers puffing over lawns.
The huge room of November
Was a home for a Massachuset
Silently crossing his brown carpet.

Along the street
Last fire,
Last gold —
Barberry fire,
Beech gold —
Flicker and glint
As dark slants on.

Closing,
She knows
A flicker,
A glint
In that dark.
There's a fire in there
Growing leaves of gold.

Night is very long.
I have slept even in the day.
I have slept even through the spring.
Even in November
New flowers are fresh.
The blooming witchhazel freshens
Above its failing leaves.
The rose is as fresh and white as the threatening snow.

She feels the flower of fire
In the sunset of late autumn
Before the astrology begins,

Before the Saracen princess Fleurdefeu
Can utter her predictions of victory and defeat.
The fire and the flower are victory.

If light ensues, if fruits
Lie piled in the cellars, if cold
Skips on the borders, a document

May enter the tradition. If a feeling
Bloomed, a vision burned, an autumn
Echoed for a moment, she fared well.

Oh, cut it out, shouts the jay.
Ah, remember that friend
Of Mother and Dad's who knew Sandscript?
Oh, remember how the el
At a certain spot used to bite its tail
Almost? Ah, remember tonsils
And the taste of wood? Oh, remember
Writing in the moist and salty sand?

Now she'll cut out
A contemporary temple
In compartments. Segments,
Sections, cuttings, clippings
Constitute her bricks; for instance,
The universe is smaller than we thought.
We thought there was a hotter fire.
We thought of a gleam beyond the massed atoms of the stars.

Post no bills,
It said on the gray sky.

Now she'll settle for a temple of bricks,
But then a temple of marble,
Then the showy echo of Pentelicus
Will rise around her as she climbs the steps
Up to the desired sidereal sheen.
Now it is possible to consider
To what music it will then be possible to hearken,
For what kudos it will then be possible to scavenge.
Caveat desiderator. Yet
The temple is loved for itself.
She surely can't help it if its acoustics
Are those of the mountains and the constellations.

So many oh's have turned into ah's.
There's one in the deodar, timber of the gods
Of Kamet and Kangra and Kew,
Of Karakoram and California.

The desideratrix
Can consider
The bricks.

It's easier to see
On a cloudy day
Looking out of

A dirty window
When it's too cold
To sit outside.

Some are redder,
And some are browner.
The day is browner.

Up to a certain height
The brown veins cling
Though the red drops are gone.

Their new storm windows
Are richly edged with brown.
They'll keep warm.

Her radiator is sputtering,
The grayed frames around her panes sag,
As she sits in her brown study.

Watch out,
You're staring south-east,
And it's morning.

What was the world,
What was herself,
And what was God
She now sits with closed eyes
And sees. The sparrows scrape their violins,
The radiator pipes up through its piccolo,
The drumsticks of the clock tap on, mutually tapping.
What was the green world,
What was her purple self,
What was the blueness of divinity
She now discovers achromatic
Against the orange of her eyelids.
The soprano of the refrigerator rises.
Scales fall from the ceiling.
I see men like trees but walking about.
Since these enchanting lineaments
Wait for her scrutiny, she looks.
The trees are a tree. The men are a man.
The slow kaleidoscope
Accepts her focus. The tree fills the screen.
It is not a tree. It is a dance.
Its beat beats in her chest,
Incarnates itself throughout her flesh.
Immovable, she feels it move.
When the dancer lays hands upon her eyes
She sees the subject of the motionless rhythm.
In the beginning, before there was movement, this dance was packaged,
And since this idol, unwrapped, exists, she surrenders.
She hears its speaking in her ears
Above the fluting of the police car,
Below the saxophoning of the truck,
Beyond the tenor of the airplane like an angel in the sky.

If the vehicle were the tenor
She would understand those who said:
Too many trees. Too florid. Too much chrome.
The trees composed an alphabet. The words
Loomed larger, like forests. The sentences . . .
Meaning shimmered through the vast
Aposiopesis. On the gold-fringed oak
She sought the fresh red drop that antedated the acorn.
The vehicle was the tenor.
The tree was trusty and true.
The dryad was its coeval.
She was the druid who saw the oak.
It was that pin oak, Quercus palustris,
Seen in that place, seen on that day and that.

It was not a good time
For seeing the oak—
The anniversary of the murder.
He had dragged her into the park.
He left her stripped and shot.
Thanksgiving weekend, people said,
Everyone out of town.
The potentate went on to live his life.
But the traffic must have kept passing
At four-thirty on a Saturday afternoon.
One is always shutting out the traffic.

November is not the time
For this oak. The oak has speckled the grass
With its brown scraps. It sticks up colorless,
Cracked, and knobby into a spotty sky.
A blue jay lays harsh, confident claim
To its heights. The gray gains timbre,
Inevitably gets to ascend in the center
Of the green lawn. It gets to be a monody
With ramifications, with sky-domed fine
Filamental resonances.
They do almost fly off in the end,
But the mass is material, rooted, trim.
Behind, the colorful traffic gives
A diffident accompaniment. From the strewn green plane
Through the solid tight-bound trunk
To the explicit linearities of the tips
An integral, an ultimate . . . Who is this capped character
That has seated himself, twiddling his thumbs,
Between me and my contemplation?

Poor Flora. What does she need?
A little clapboard shuttered house
In the suburbs, a little back yard,
A flowery patch, a tree or two
Within the fence? Purdah,
Claustration? Does Little Red Riding Hood need
A chaperon, a chape, a coat of mail?

A remembered temple in a remembered sky.
A remembered temple in an actual sky.
An actual temple in a remembered sky.
These are possible. But it's too cold
For too much actuality. Either your windows
Are streaked or your eyes water. And it's too bright,
Too early on the eve of Advent for a hymn
To the dews of heavens past. The sparrows

Have just relinquished their harping. Then set
The actual in the remembered. Ignore
Your bricks splashed on the opposite windows.

The old red blanket had been spread out on the slats.
Maybe it wasn't old then. Once it must have been new.
The sky was new. It surpassed Manhattan.
It stretched beyond ken and kenning,
Earth-holder, eye-opener, edge-toucher, mind-rouser.
Tall buildings whirl. Straight lines waver. Parallels crash.
It stays there, smoothly deepening. Build while it's still,
Still ô ciel azur, ó céu azul.

A blue background. That will do for a while.
Branching in a December dusk,
On late azure, on early rose.
That will do. A sudden shift
To greenest Florida or greenest June
With brightest flittings. That will serve.
We suppose—superpose—the same sky,
Turning the lights up or down,
Filling or clearing the stage.

Branches are cut in the watchet
Letting the black show through
And the black is punctured with gleams
Like Manhattan from the Esplanade at night
And the stars come rushing to the boughs
Not like sparrows, not like eagles,
Like suns volleying to earth.

We thought our dominoes were cities,
And they fell as bowling pins fall.

A quieter version. A sky of prussian blue.
The black December branches cold and clear.
Or something like this. Design without design.
A urobore. A Celtic decoration.
Decus. Something like this. Here it is.

O fortunate whose cities rise!
In a grove in the center at the crest of the hill
You begin to see against the sky,
As she points, the bronzen portals hoisted,
The marble metopes carved and hued.

The child sat in relief with her knees drawn up,
Her little marble fingers clasped around them.
She seemed to rest against niello stripes.
Her eyes of lapis lazuli looked out,
Her face tilted up. And whence is this to me?
VISITATIO was the inscription.

The next read DURA. A marble oak
Would never shed its emerald leaves
In mere November. Slender nymphs
Dancing in green around the tree
Were tougher than duramen, strong
As stone, unchipped, unbrokenhearted.

Tyrian birds in a Mycenaean sky,
Three purple birds that sing in a sky of gold,
Like a trio of strings that sound in a golden hall,
Shimmer and glide over CONTEMPLATIO, cutting across wide
Space, through long time, and no wings rise or fall
And no bows swiftly shift or slowly hold
Before the blinking of the augur's eye.

Above CAUTA, like a cardinal that clicks
Through the chill into the December sun,
A slim woman in a ruby dress
Of velvet was bent over cuneiform,
Impressing what she had observed, for the fire
Reddened well within the frame.

On the blank but candid panel gleamed a star,
And then a twin appeared, and soon a third,
And then a fourth, and soon a constellation
Was sprayed like orange sunrise. Then the wise,
Amazed, were gazing, saying: Where is he?
Carved letters spelled DESIDERATIO.

5. Season

Boots are pulled on.
The sun stops.
It is called winter.

Snow is refashioning New England.
Snow has halted New York.
Snow has glittered all day across the Plains and over the Rockies.
Along the Pacific there's nothing but precipitation.

Here the bugs sang all last night.
Only the writhing cajeputs are white.
Under the ramrod palms you stroll in sandals through the evening light.

6. Tree

The etymology, the genuine speech,
Here stutters. But the Malay derivation
Is given: cajeput, white tree.
The Austronesian roots don't speak to me.
These trees seem rootless, seem to stand
On the close-clipped grass as in an opaque
Green mere. You'd think their feet were
Planted on a shallow, unseen bottom.
And still they're flourishing, though far from home.
Florida, said Flora, is the land of flowers.

From the screened porch, with its seasonable
Show of red and green—blooming
Christmas cactus, poinsettias with subtended
Inflorescence, tannenbaum with its suspended
Efflorescence, among the watering cans—
Beyond a square of screen, beyond the glare
Of the parking lot, across the glint of the road,
In the ample stripe of green beside
The path along the gold wall in front of the gold
Buildings, silver-balconied, bronze-tile-roofed
(Discreetly gold the buildings, the long wall, refined,
Although the sky is indiscreetly blue,
Blazingly, unblushingly, insistently noon-blue
In cloudless noon over stiff gold buildings), you see
The cajeputs with fuzzy tops,
With feathery, green-gray-haired heads
Lost in whitish cloudlets, with white thighs
Discreetly white. We walked along the path
Beside the line of cajeputs, along the path, along…

The trunks are finger-painted in high relief;
The foliage is brush-painted, with the vagueness
Of the brush; the flowers, from the porch, no longer
Brushes, no longer clouds, are stars. We had seen
And were come. One bole
Was straight and single, another
A couple relaxed at a cocktail party, a third
A ménage à trois (quite comfortable), a fourth,
Fifth, sixth, and seventh a loving or warring
Crossing and conjoining of enormous limbs. Through the grid
The cajeputs are wrapped below, stellar
Above, palaestral below, adagio above, earthy
Below, airy above, fleshly
Below, spirit above, at last

Shadow below, sunlight above,
White shade, green-gilded sun.
We walked along the path, along the path, along
The line of cajeputs in their attitudes.

7. Sky

I admit it. This flat land
Supports a lot of sky. The road
Is stretched out like a tape measure, inched along

At the rush hour, lined with white cubes,
Gold cubes, pink cubes, cubes of powder blue,
With Australian pine, pandanus, palm, and poinciana.

Otherwise, sky. Similarly,
Over the bay. You walk down the lawn
Past the live oaks, the banyan, the gumbo limbo,

The two sedate date palms, the solemn
Avenue of royal palms, to where the last
Lone coconut palm leans out insouciant over the water.

Whitely the egret steps fastidiously by.
Blackly the cormorant spreads his wings to dry.
On a pole the pelican yawns an enormous brown yawn

Above the pink and blue endless ripple.
Blast that airplane, and that, and that.
But how did I get here?

The boom and buzz of this great bee
Through the sky. Bright blossoms of stars
Are still very distant. The sky
Is still very distant. It stands apart,
Holding its flowers. O tell me, Fleurdefeu,
How did we get here? The yellow grass,
The diminishing city, the small silver boxes,
The gray mist, the white mist,
The burst into blue above the white beach,
White desert, white vaporous ocean,
White monstrous snowfather. Dazzle
Beams up from the back of the cloud mass, not
From the higher, unlined, elemental face
Still gazing down from wherever its owner
Has backed off to. The clouds, says the man in the moon,
Are part of the earth. And I see the streaming black locks
Of your vaunted heaven. Which still gapes down
From wherever...O tell me, Fleurdefeu,

How cold is it here, how strong is the wind,
How thin is the air? Through the interference
Of double panes, the static of plastic and glass,
The monoscopic reception, I catch
A far sky, a flat sky,
A painted sky. Skies like trees
Blunt in paintings. But this scene is crayoned
In kindergarten: at the lower edge
Of the page, the strip of brown; at the upper edge
Of the paper, the stripe of blue; in the blank between,
Our silvery flight. Our shadow winged
Across the tops of the clouds, but the clouds are gone.
The dazzle is gone. We can stare out up
At the upper air. We peer down at Cape Fear,
Sharp, unmistakable, mapped, a mark.
The movie comes on. Please draw the blinds.
Next, stars glint far above and below
Our starless sail. To a gazer in a starry window
Below, our wingtips twinkle. Wherever we are
Is starless. We're held in the arms of the sky,
At arm's length, the face of the sky
Where it always was. We're sitting apart
Holding our arms, holding our flowers.

We flew east into sunrise through the night.
We flew south into summer through December.
Spring began again and again as we leapt northward.
We flew west from June and landed on January ice.
We captured miles of years in a glance from heaven.
Hibiscus by a white wall in this hot sun;
The distant recognized white straight gleam
Of the World Trade Center two inches high;
The bright, blue, cold Januarial sky
Behind the winter-lit branches.
The blue nuthatches, the chickadees, the creepers hold the trunks.
The juncos, the cardinals, the blue jays win the boughs.
The stiff gray alate beast drones its mastery over the air.
Epiphany is blue and clear. The first cracks show
In the armor of the witchhazel. Visible on the frozen pond
Are fallen leaves, thrown rocks, cracked sky.

8. Tree

The American elk and the American elm
Both have foreign names which suit them
Well enough, if, indeed, to the Proto-Indo-Europeans
Jabbering away in their smoky huts
During cold Caucasian winters, el
Meant red or brown. To the Proto-Indo-Americans
It was the white spot on their elk that mattered,
That gave it a name. Wapiti, they called it.
It wasn't an elk, of course, but a deer.
Their elk they called moose. Their deer
Someone dreaming of home named elk.
And what mattered on their elm?

February. The shadow seen.
Some white spots seen
Along the brown ridges of the elm.
The bold, barren shadow is stretched
Along the red bricks of the temple.

The shadow slips by.
No time for watching.
Short days. A short month. A short
Shadow. A short, cold time.

The grammar of winter is scratched
In diagrams. A squirrel is sucking
Icicles. Branches are adjectives ascribed
To the sky. Up there a squirrel is munching
Twiglets. The invention of the elm,
However, releases a rhetoric.
There's a Helen here, a Heracles here,
Beyond the unfluted columns, the flat
Metopes, the empty pediment.
Cassandra's wild arms rise as cries
Flash under gold guttae—the golden drops.
Apollo bends, turning tips to gold.
Reason meets dream.
Lines are persuasion.

If it weren't February it would
Be March. In no month in no year
Osiris was born.
The buds are bigger.
The periods soon will be commas,
Semicolons, question marks, shoots
Of exclamation.

In the temple, for the image of the god,
Stands a bowl of flowers resembling

The branches of the elk,
The antlers of the elm.

9. Season

I would not think of committing
The pathetic fallacy. I would not think
Of thinking the impluviation
Of the second day of spring
Was a sign (either symbol or symptom)
Of cloudy things about the heart
And behind the eyes or of what those clouds
Could do, she thought with a dim, dull thought,
Unstormily, without precipitation.
If the sun had smiled she might have had to weep.
But even when the rain stopped gilding the yellow grass
All the slivered crocuses flinched
As a wind circled loud as a plane,
Now in an attempt to land,
Now with an intent to bomb.
A few white pellets,
A few garnet-blossomed silver boughs
Began the bombardment. Landed,
That wind, automobilized, dashed
Through every red light.
Yesterday it was different.

Spring was her Achilles' heel,
She thought, clicking the cliché
Along the sidewalk. Higher heels
Are in again. Click, click. Cliché.
Achilles' heel. Hero
She was none, but well she knew
That once you've crossed the Rubicon
Each and every victory must be Pyrrhic
Except the last. Achilles' heel:
A double pain. They always get you in the spring.
Once Thetis or the obstetrician held you
With thumb and finger like tongs,
Dipping you, except for two small spots,
Into Stygian life. They always get you in the spring:
Alexander or Apollo,
Scylla or Charybdis,
The devil or the deep blue sea.

They sing you a siren song.
They offer you Pandora's box.
They turn down a Procrustean bed for you.
You can't turn it down.

She looked at the Procrustean bed.
Embroidered in pink on the pillow she read:
Get your act together. She found it odd
To be embroidered

Though the thread did not seem to be dangling much
From the needling words.

She looked into Pandora's box.
A bird cheeped: Hopefully, the sky at equinox
Can also be unlocked. The hopeful one
Had a sinking feeling

Though happily, presumably, most fortunately the sky
Was not yet falling.

She looked from where she was afloat
To where they sang. She rocked the boat.
Was she so clever, had she such friends,
That she'd stay and cling

Though the call came ever clearer: Come
To us and sing?

Apollo, sunny singer, my destroyer,
Feverish whirlpool, deepest sea,
And what they will not believe.
I cannot make them believe
That march of the god
Through the march of March:
The enraged leonine entrance
To the witchhazel's re-clenched fists
That had sunnily spread benediction with incense
Above the late snow before the late frosts
(The epitaph of the crocus said:
Born in February, died in March —
A brief cold life in a trap of the sun);
Then the cardinal's cheering, the woodpecker's drumming,
The crow's crowing as he shook his black cloak
From the whitish summit of the sycamore
(Coming, coming, coming through the cold);
The reopening, the second crocuses,
The glints of green in the yellow grass
(Waiting, waiting, waiting for April);
The March snow sweeping
Along the black street,
The blue snow sleeping
Beneath the black trees;
Sun, an open window, beyond the traffic
A call: Phoebe, phoebe — not to the moon,
To the song of Phoebus, Phoebean aoedé,
La chanson

D'Apollon
Que nous écoutons.
Spring-resonant, sun-resplendent, the cardinal high in the maple,
A sheer incarnadine against sheer blue,
Flaunts our triumph over winter.

Winter is always with us.
Winter lurks in the spring:
Get and store,
Look aft and fore,
There's a monster soon,
There's a devil at noon,
To gulp your tune.
Watch the wintry arrow of the springborn Alexander.

Man or god will get you in the spring.
You may sacrifice the sun to entrenched and heroic grubbing,
You may sacrifice your fruit to eternal divine floration,
Between the devil and the deep blue sky.

The mockingbird sang through the rain.
The robin sang in an outburst of ruddy sun.

Not a red-breasted robin at all;
A deceiving American migratory thrush.
Shall I migrate, muse,

To hear the nightingale this spring,
To watch the wing-sweet swan,
To rent a windowed room? There's a vacancy
Among the lower Parnassian rocks.

10. Temple

In this room the clock has stopped.
Its silent face reflects like a moon.
A floral design in the carpet
Reflects designs beyond the bay window:
Flowers, stars. A full-faced moon,
As we sat all night under rough red blankets,
Accompanied our unresting flight toward dawn
With a constant gaze through the little curve of the window
And with, as though from the ocean, an answering
Gleam like perfume from the unflowered, unstarred carpet beyond the window,
The old gray rumpled blanket of cloud below us.
The clock has stopped. Out in the garden
The old cat lies among the flowers
That last as the June days last,
As the blackbird's utterance lasts and lasts
Among the jewelled lilacs, over the glistering golden
Fleece of laburnum, along the stone walls. From the golden beak
The song flows, ripples, eddies, crashes on the rocks.

Through the splashes, through the flaps,
The wings of the swan ring over the silver waters.
Blue drops of speedwell bloom on the bank.
A northern island, Flora thought, is the land of flowers,
Indigo, violet, red, orange, gold, in a June of green
Freshened by the faithful clouds. Yet, Fleurdeleau,
The sun is reaching with a very long arm around the curve of the world.

O fortunate.

The wapiti now is nearly extinct
Over much of the United States. Before
The decline of the American elm its boughs
Were selected as sites for well-woven nests
By New World northern orioles—not
Orioles, of course, and yet
Clear goldfish of the American sky.

O lucky one
Who has begun.

In a land of orioles and lilacs—
Orange and lavender, sweet and clear—
She followed the scent of lilacs,
She followed the oriole call through the afternoon,
The flagrant flash through the afternoon sun,
On and on, moving on and on.
As the lavenders glistened into dusk,
Lavenders pure or lush or ethereal—
Lilac bush, wistaria vine, and princess tree—
She attended the woodthrush song through the evening,
The subtle invitation spaced with silence,
From a dark thicket, summoning to night.

O fortunate few
Whose walls are new
Under skies of blue.

The loud clock in the back room can be moved.
Now there is only the soft ticking of rain
And medium ticking of sparrows, with blackbird chimes.
The door is open into the back garden.
Traffic buzzes now and then, remote and weak.
In the strong house of stone—not clapboard, not brick—no radiator emits
Geysers toward a flaking ceiling
Or sprinkles a warped wooden floor.
She is not hastily moving clay tablets;
The showers fall outside. She buttons her red sweater.
The door is open to let in a little warmth,
But she is not looking out into the garden

And jumps up only to re-route a wasp.
A tablet lies under her hand. Where she looks
No color exists unless for an instant
The dull red wool. This is the unclocked time
To hear the involutions of the deep red rose of thunder.

Edging the thunder, entering the rose,
Slipping to the center of the burning woodthrush phrase,
Without a movement, in a rest wrung from movement,
Like the rest between two phrases—
Sometimes it is easy,
Sometimes is it impossible,
Sometimes it is meaningless. The meaning
Is there and is not there. For example,

The swan floats into the sunset.
The meaning floats far into the sunset
Before the thoughts, before the words,
Before the syllables are launched.
There at the edge of meaning he swerves.
If he should turn, return, storm
The still waters, fly
For her mind, she might glide
Out to the red sun, attain the thunder,
Enter. She did. She heard
The meaning. The woodthrush phrase
Curved around her. She
Curved around it. She could
Feel, like a wizened thin-fingered crone,
Among the rosy involutions; she could
Slide, like an eager rose-cheeked child,
To focus. Ah: the syllable
First said by the infant, last made
By the old aphasiac, solely sung
In the concerto for coloratura soprano
And orchestra. Keu: part of the ancestral
Word. Hear: part of the thought
Within the petals of the song.

If you were painting the three blatant oranges in the glass dish
Each would be daubed with a region of sunlit peaks
And shaded beyond the terminator. Within the crystalline ellipse
You would chart degrees, discover poles,
Fix the dark curve of one sphere on another.
If you surveyed the reiterated flowers on the papered wall
You would measure the cloud, the hour, the damascene
Angle painting and repainting
Petals brighter and darker than their orange centers.

Desire has its intonations. Do you remember
The orange and black of the oriole's imperative,
The orange sun at the heart of the sleek black tulip,
The sweep of the vast orange slide
On undulant meadows of lawn
Somewhere not far from the ocean
In the darkening of an August night?
That was the unmapped place
To desire the apricot sunning on the blackened bough
When from the blackened heavens
The constellations were calling.

The words of that sidereal call
Shone sharp and clear. But when you began
To transcribe them from a page of sky
You could not scratch so deep as they were high.
Oh: the longing of November wind.
Sweid: the swish of the leafy stars.
Desire: the valley and the hill.

Past the firebush,
Cornered by purple and gold I stopped.
Here I found it.

The slope seemed a bit unpropitious
And the big laburnum tree leaned so far
That the gardeners had reined it to the hillside.
But glimpsed behind the atropunic beech
Or watched from by the aurifoliate privet
The laburnum reared, gold tassels tossing,
Over the lavender breakers of rhododendron.
And so I cut my trapezoid through the air,
Posting at its unquestionable fines
Bush and tree and bush and tree,
Golden, purple, purple, gold,
Gold and purple leaves,
Purple and golden flowers.

Tesk and temple be before me.

                              Bounded by words
It had risen through the numinous mist
Waiting for contemplation, waiting for golden
Eagles to quarter the hillside, soar,
Soar, glide. Sheer rays of sun
Shone above the puffed purpureal clouds
As the great laburnum king above
The regal rhododendron. Free
From tint of red, both multitudinous
Lemon rods and lavender spheres

Pursued, like fixed stars, once the wind
Had rested, their unmoving course
Across the afternoon, beyond
The bright gleams of the privet,
The dark glints of the beech.
A golden mouth was moving in the tree,
A purple throat was moving by the bush.

Tem: The big fish cuts like a golden sword
Through the reflection of the purple iris.
Contemplate: The waiting iris shines
Unmoved above the mirroring pool.

When you looked from the large central window
Or opened the strong iron gate
You would glance at the small blue flower on the small white rock
And think that tomorrow,
And think that when the sky turned white and blue
You would burst into the sapphire of the morning
To view the flower on the rock.
Tomorrow a gray wind swooped from an old gray sky,
Or was it the old gray cat,
Or the old gray gentleman with his scythe?
The flower lay below the rock.

When you brought the little thing into the front parlor
You could see five-petaled perfection in the thimble of water
And remember the blue gaze gazing south from the rock
As you hurried from breakfast,
And remember forget-me-nots sprinkled by the swan-suave lake
As you ran to lunch,
And remember the Arabian swirl of blue smoke
Of ceanothus on the daisied hillside
As you rushed to supper,
And remember Dad's smooth hands in the funeral parlor.

An actual temple in a remembered sky:
This is possible. You can sow
White virgin columns in the rock
Below that clear blue. Wid: see.
Weid: have seen and know.
View: if not then, why not now?

Like the round head of a pin
Or a small seed above the rock
Yesterday the lithospermum
Bud gleamed hard and green,
As she stooped, in the little garden. In a vast garden,
The day before, in a northern Athens, the Himalayan
Deodar, like a green-feathered eagle, like a green-shagged peak
Gleamed, as she sat, with a distant misty Parthenon under its wing.

This is not our music. Ours,
Of more than spears that wing over mountains,
Of broken nuclei, trodden moons,
Beeps, crackles, tleers, and zooms.
Pandora's little hope
Goes up in smoke.

Where there is no affirmation
There are no lies. The bud softened.
The deodar poised like a deer
Or like a kitten that she wanted to stroke.
The moon above the Himalayas
Gleamed. The misty north sky darkened.
The lightning spared the tree.
She ran indoors and turned the key
And watched the storm through glass and spoke:
Deru: the acorn and the oak.
Doru: strength stronger than the spear.
Trust: if not there, why not here?

O lucky one
Who has begun
To build in the sun.

The only tree was the telephone pole
With its branches, the oversized bridge
Of the vast violin strung above the long arm
Of the street and bowed by the resident
Sparrow: Hear me, hear me, hear me,
Outside the grayish window
Of the brick apartment house. Hello,
Hello. Hear me, hear me.

O fortunate few
Whose walls are new.

The bees buzzed back, officially announcing
A universe no longer ananthous.
It was time to do her tenth symphony
In the vowelless syllables of Bella Coola.
Green grass, one week miraculous,
The next week was taken for granted.
It was time for temples, epics, festivals,
Lawns and lawnmowers,
Leaves and the shadows of leaves.
A fragrance in a stray wind
Was of the scents that are remembrances:
Evenings of robin and apple blossom,

The forbidden beauty of the rosebud cherry,
Innocent as a child's kisses.
The breeze flowed through the bars
Of the fire escape. O Fleurdefeu,
Tell her it is time to solmizate
April's orange elms,
May's pink oaks,
The vibrant white of dogwood on dark
Hemlock. The innocent breeze
Went whispering down the lanes,
Was pushed down narrow lanes between
Skyscrapers. Prohibited strains
Seeped from the short American spring.
But during the expanding afternoon
Below the silver maple's bloody flowers
She had drowned in the deep blue squills.

O luck.

The little clock is ticking. The wind
Calls Wish in the leaves and Want in the chimney.
Ears are lidless. At the sharp gray peak
Of the Empire State Building when it was Everest
Of buildings, wind suspired thus, circling
Auricularly yet not sweeping
Eyeglasses upstream or out to sea.
See, the river unwinds north,
The ocean unfolds into daybreaks. Go
As the wind goes. The old red blanket
Billows on the slats. Liftoff. Everest.
Evenings of green, rose, marble,
Eagles, skies, evenings of skies.

ii. Season

At midnight we walked out toward the sea,
Leaving our teacups beside the peat fire.
The silvery ground of the sky
Displayed some orange and purple tracks
Left by the scarlet slug that had slipped into the north.
Two shadows circled sirening
Gently. We blinked at the striking
Of giant matches on headlands and islands.
From glinting tracks the endless train
Of the sea kept sounding.
We pulled our winter coats tighter.
It was summer.

Behind us, to the east, was the hill
We climbed from the little road.
Three thousand years before, feet
Climbed the hillock, eyes
Measured the rows, firm hands
Held the slabs straight, patted the stones
Against each base, where the tormentil
Glittered gold beneath the circling
Curlew, circling lapwing, plunging
Lark, above dark purple orchids
And the lavender antlers of the ragged robin,
Above misty towers of cathedrals of the sea,
The antlers of two oil rigs. The wind came circling
Around the gray sky and plunged
Upon the cows, upon two homines sapientes standing
Between the Bronze and Petroleum Ages.

The stone rows in the grass above the North Sea
Resembled a graveyard above Narragansett Bay,
Without inscription, without Dad's date, without Dad's name.

Behind us, to the west, was the hill
We climbed from the little road.
It was bigger, and the path we tried
Was the path of a spring. When we reached the top,
Stopping for eyebright, walking among
The tormentil, hearing the curlew and the lark,
Seeing the sheep and the fields, rising above
The grassy stony mounds of the men who gave crops to the north
And chambered tombs to themselves five thousand years before,
We discovered, sharp and clear, beyond the fields, beside the sea,
Two white shapes:
A visiting, naturalized, geometrized moon,
The great white gleaming smokeless sphere
Of (already old-fashioned, outmoded, out-of-date)
The experimental fast reactor (DFR),
And beside it, issuing cloud-white draconic breath,
An anatural, geometrical, anthropometrical chunk of the globe of space,
The great white gleaming smoking solid rectangle
Of (still forerunner, still of the future, still of the about-to-be)
The prototype fast reactor (PFR).
We crossed the cairns, two bipeds stepping
From the New Stone to the Nu Clear Age.

These days never gave up their ghosts.
Silvery spirits hovered, tinged
With orange and purple, about their lips.

12. Tree

How can she remember it now—
With the blinds down, with the movie on, with the smoke drifting back,
With the intermittent clatter at the bar, with the constant
Oom of the engine, far above
The clatter and oom of the ocean,
The blinding cinematic clouds—
How in the quiet forest garden where the goldcrest fluttered
The green Caucasian fir
Pulled at the muscles of her eyes?
It was a perfect triangle, shining green, light-tipped
But dark within, pulling her eyes
Wider and wider.

13. Sky

The greenish-yellow candles of ailanthus
Lit in a gray July.
The heat of the sun without the sun,
The moisture of rain without any rain,
Encased and lined her. Sticky,
Succinctly reported the announcer.
And it was linden time. The rare
Breezelets sweetened segments of atmosphere
On the lee shore, where she wished
To be found, to be. The ailanthus
Nestled against the brick wall.

The golden candles of the rain tree
Lit the garden. Still the opaque
Gray plane of sky resisted contemplation,
Smashed the yo-yo of her vision,
Letting her almost hear the clack
Of the gray painted billboard, the clang
Of iron, the thunder over rain.

When the rainbow stretched down over the grass
She almost ran to the foot of the mountain.
Yet it was on a February afternoon,
Without grass, without mountains, without rainbows,
That she sighted the keystone of the heavens.
All the horizons were pale, but straight up, above the elm,
Smoldered that blue,
Not pale, not dark, not dull, not bright,
But deep, receptive, penetrable,
The vertex once known.
Banish the restlessness of adjectives to rest

In the temple, sink into the sky,
And kiss the light.

And here it is on the fourth of July,
Squeezed out between the leaves,
Or smeared, as she leans on the black railing,
There over the roof of the brick building
Where a single swift flits swerving,
Or sampled as a river between two elms
With a bay beyond and then an ocean
Where white fleets pass and are gone,
And the green banks of elm leaves approach her and sharpen—
The banks move while the river is still—
And the blue supernal river deepens in its channel
And, flowing green over grass between shores of shadow,
Deepens as her eyes cleave the earth
(If these—they must be, though not unmistakably—are
What that February sky, although unmistakably, was),
Or sensed—this is it—with the windows pushed up, the shades drawn over the panes,
The world seen, heard, and felt through the screens,
In the room's three-quarter summer light,
Close, here, on the books, on the chair, on the floor,
As a sparrow harps, as a bicycle fiddles,
As an airplane croons, as a bus sighs: You
Could join this light
Without parades, without firecrackers, without loud adjectivals.
Even the nouns and the verbs have begun to disappear,
Leaving infinitives.
                    N'y voir que du bleu?
Of course, there are certain predications
Sweetly breathed from the gold and purple throat
Of the fair catalpa, allegedly made
By the bittersweet nightshade of purple locks
And pointed golden tongue.
The bricks are fire-baked.
The samaras are flames.
The tree of heaven is smoke-resistant.
This sky is the empyrean.
Whether it is the sky or some eagle beating
In herself or, shadowed among the sand dunes, herself,
With the shore lost, with the sun lost,
With the wet grass knifing her knees,
This fire goes on burning.
Here is an escape.

The Sheen

1. Troy

Apart. Where the gold.
At lunch. O forget it.
But that's. Well, not now.
The issues. Not now.
Apart, where the gold-lined wings
Were actions, were wings of words
Louder than actions, were silences
Louder than words, she sat
In the afternoon's deserted field
By the edge of the thicket. In the trees
Bronze birds with gold-lined wings
Were sometimes leaves, were sometimes
What they were. The leaves flickered.

Bronze and gold, the words fluttered
Into mown autumn. At lunch.
Forget it. Not those words. Silence
Dappled the grass. Apart.
The aspen crowds were cheering, waving
Their hands, their handkerchiefs, jingling coins
In their pockets. Fire-engine cardinals
Broke for the scarlet camouflage now
Proffered by the euonymus. The Ionian white and gold
Of the birches lined the portico. Apart.
She couldn't work anyway, with all that noise
From the maple. The archangelic sky
Trumpeted out of its distances pure
Blue glories. Not allowed.

Prohibited: one golden glimpse
Without that, there, or then.
One golden glimpse. Finding a camp chair,
She dragged it over. Here was the sky,
Here the maple, here the grass
Filling again with robins, here
The wood, and here the hill.

Up the hill someone was painting
A poignancy of red, the aureolation of orange,
Those kingly purples, on a green canvas.
Let it be something manly, Jack,
Something virile, something of authentic virtue,
Not these ecstasies of autumn, sunset,
Triple rainbows beyond the ridge,
Waning slices of moon beyond
The birches. And yet ascent
Is easiest. How your moccasined feet
Lope up the rocks while your eyes deny
All but crest and sky.
Your toes are pinched, your knees out of joint
As you slouch back down. I paint what I see
And always in natural light, with gloves
If needed: hues, tunes, weathers,
Tints, shades, shadows,
Shadows, caverns as of clouds,
De profundis surfaces,
Surfaces, species. A breeze
Sent gold and crimson leaves like fallen angels in facile ascent
Toward their old places on high.

You can't see it? It was surfaces she loved,
Yet she hovered at edges, which suggested depths
Without requiring penetration. The irrelevant
Butterflies glittered near her in the field;
Flashing significance, the flickers flicked
At the tips of the thicket. Meanings like those
Of a green island in a stream,
Of a white island in an ocean,
Reached her eyes as she sat in the enormous clearing
Watching, to the cicadas' orchestration,
Past the goldenrod and Queen Anne's lace,
The stage where action glimmered among the columns of the trees.
There's something there.
But under the klieg afternoon
All the birds stopped playing their parts.

One golden glimpse. She turned to the maple.
Here was perfect surface and sure
Dimension curving behind the facade.
The sextant of her gaze
Adjusted to the shock of scarlet
And all the orpiments. She recognized
The tones of reality, away
From the usual unreal. She understood
The parallax of reality, apart

From the real club sandwiches, headlines, companionate
Mutterings. She gobbled the communion.
Far from the cry of battle and the rhetoric of the assembly
Where men reel in glory she listened
To messages other than the shadows, as the gold-tongued maple
Spoke, with undertones of viridity,
With overtones of bronze bells clanging,
In releasing rhythms, of angles
Of satisfaction: slanting
Panting almost, sharp red now,
And coppery reflection; the climb, the top,
The symphony in the resounding valley,
Mosaics for them to walk on, to dig up,
To reconstruct; matter only
Holding form, only emitting
Energy, only accepting
The ears' fierce grasp,
The eyes' slow fiery osculation.

Because it was quite enough
Or because it was not quite enough,
The intersection of tree and sky
Seemed the clearest clear, the truest
Gold, the happiest blue. And wading out
From the bright strand into the bright
Azure she began to feel
On ankles, on thighs, on shoulders the eternal
Swirl, the eternal pull.
Is there a tide in the sky?
Is there an undertow in the sky?

No, you can't say these things.
You can't say any of these things.
But what were they saying at lunch? You've got
To do something? Actions, they said.
Well, you know that women weigh less
On pay scales. Gosh, two nights in a row?
Well, just a scare. You know
That women are night's booty. But what
Did they say he said? Well, words
Will never. Apart. Where the gold.

Down the blue Kennebec we came,
Pushing our way around the rocks
Before we could pack the water into dams,
The soil under rails, the soil into lanes
For thruways, the soil into strips
Under airways. Up the brown Kennebec we flew.

The sun set, and the saints' dark bodies
Stepped up into the light, stood
In the glass. From the dark she saw them.

The green and yellow and orange translucent
Around them, sectioned, simpler than the deepening
Darkening sunset of the maple,

Gave them their own plainer, flatter,
Not less luminous, more enduring
October as an environment

In which their stance, solemn, almost
Opaque, was inviting, promised the high
White wax aflame—

Peaks of radiance, flowing and rippling
Rivers of song, mists as sweet
As ten June evenings, and, sweeter,

The secret taste of God on the tongue,
Down the throat, in the breast. Then all heads bowed.
Heavy the incense hung.

We made it here on that eighteen-seater
That tosses you over and over the billows of air,
Or stacked our stuff in a U-Haul and tugged
It up in spite of five hours gasped second
By second across the George Washington Bridge,
Or survived the unventilated hold of the Greyhound bus
Becalmed before clearing Boston.

Turning away, she walked down apart from the clutter of people
By the white sea foam, looking out over the wine-shaded deepness,
Praying aloud, with her hands stretched over the glittering water.
Far in the distance the four white ships went on sailing together.

Across the lake the four white swans sailed on
In smooth and silent beauty. Yet one smashed
Against that yielding element: he crashed
His forces on the surface; splashed great sprays
Into receptive air; in might was gone,
Received along the singing, flashing ways.

Across the pond the four white ducks
Progressed in order, by mute rules
And uttered regulations. Grass,
For her the last solidity,
Had launched them. From the dry and firm
Terrestrial slope her arms reached forth
Above the level, yielding, stirring
Spread. The steeple rippled down.

That bounded, unending liquidity, where her steps stopped,
That alien pliancy past the margin where she walked
Shadowed itself brightly on the tree trunks, where the light
Flexed. Like long-haired Achaeans, the willows
Stood strong and comely. Like gods, the willows
Swished their silver ambrosial locks, turned gold
As the chryselephantine anatids sank on the gilded hill.
And from where the fowl had been laboring on the shore
A hundred swans, a thousand gleaming ships
Crossed the wide water, prows forward, sails proud,
To be beached among the bottles. Dotted
With gold the warblers darted out.

Catch a bug.
Catch a fish.
Catch a god.
Like an anhinga, the warbler
Was shaking his wetted wings.

The silvery willows reached out, touching
The silvery waters. The watery willows
Reached the willowy waters. The silvery
Surfaces touched. The willowy silvers
Met the silvery willows. The watery
Silvery willows met the waters.
The surfaces touched. And Flora knew,
When the ducks stopped gossiping, how easy it would be
For someone sitting by a gray-bearded father,
Someone willowy, watery, silvery,
Someone silver-footed swiftly to plunge
Up from the sunken inverted weather-vane ship.

The pond went rushing with the wind
Faster and faster to the inevitable edge.
A silvery chill came gliding across the water,
Insinuating eld into the gray beards of the willows.
The wind blew up a cerulean ocean
Lined with the repetitive signposts of the trees.
Down upon the ducks came floating
Feathers of the firstling snow.
What weathercock trees.
The elegant willowy tresses have thinned.
She's walking on hairs.
They crackle, as the ducks crackle, on the grass.
They lie by the duckless pond in the soundless snow.
When were the sails unfurled?
When were the oars pushed down?
Beyond the yellowish, diminished willows

The still, thick pond is obdurate. The frozen ripples
Never shift. No one now will get through.
There, testing the ice, stands a gull
That has beaten in from the distant ocean.

2. Ithaca

Neither stay-at-home Penelope
Nor cute little Nausicaa
Nor that bitch Calypso
Nor Helen at forty playing the gracious hostess
Back in Sparta with her starry-eyed husband
Nor sister Clytemnestra the killer
Nor certainly Circe for all her aplomb
But the Muse-sung male was her hero:
The role-model, the archetype, the star.
Male me in tell Muse much turning.
What hero ever stayed at home
Or, like Nausicaa, did the wash
At an outdoor laundromat or crazed
Men into bestiality? Tell me, Muse,
What do you think?

When there was no longer a pond
But only a white slope and a white plain
And the wind built a white mountain on the plain
And a hand planted a stick on the mountain
Like an oar to Neptune, it was time to depart.

A numb hand clutched the handle of her tote bag full of books.
She was stepping down the white hill like an egret wearing boots.
Nevertheless, when she reached the bridge,
She saw him/her as he/she stood
Backed by black pines, white birches, gray alders
On a white shore beside the black waters.
Seek past gray but never suppose
There is only the beachhead where you stand or only
An elusive current coursing through night.
The moon rustled in the stream.
The dry snow shone.

Down the white Kennebec she flew,
Then between flights slid into a cab
And skidded off to check some footnotes.
Then, as the elevator redescended, there he was
In his soft gray suit. Hi! Which way? Down.
Which way were they going? The cage
Dropped quickly around her heart.

His gray locks shocked her. They were thick, though,
And his gray eyes electric. Then they stared
At his glistening boots and her sodden loafers.
Time for a cup of coffee? No. But thanks.
The wet snow hung heavy on the yews.
A gray squirrel clung to the garbage basket grate.
She cleared the slush. The taxi splashed off.

Then they were spraying the smoking icy wings.
Then. Then. Then. The bump,
The braked run, the stiff stumbling
Walk, the dizzying watch, the turning
Luggage, thump. Then the warm
Moist breeze, the green, the green.

Sun showered the umbrella tree
And dripped from its glistening domes
As frisbees whirled like discuses
And happy voices called her in.
Here's the bath, and here's the feast,
And here are our newest songs.
Tell us now about your trip.

I shouldn't have said that
About Calypso. She was kind to me.
But she wanted me to forget
The fires blue burning above
My Ithaca. Her soft
Words, her soft... But this is the end
Of my story.

           The beginning?
From the bay their four white arms
Kept flashing as they swam to the green
Slope of the lawn. Did they see me
As I sat by a palm tree that rattled
Like raindrops rattling on a roof?

Above the roof the vultures'
Black and sun-tan wings
Sidled closer and closer, but wind
Filled with sun was sweeping sweetly
Across the green. The wind was a sea
In the shells of my ears as I stood up and walked
On the stubbly grass, on the spongy grass.
There was no grassy grass. The pelicans
Flopped, the palm feathers flapped, the pelicans
Flipped, the palm fingers clicked.
The squeaks of the gulls, the bray of the jay,
The protestations of the parrot

Greeted the singers singing on the shore.
The wind whispered across the water.
The sun screamed across the water.

As far away the sun is playing
His icicle lyre, so the wind here fingers
The harpstrings of the palm, they sang,
And we sing to you. Female, woman,
We will not break you on the rocks where the bones
Whiten in the sun. Those are men's bones.
Woman, female, with us you will sing
On the grass among the purples of the butterfly trees.

The fish were swimming in the air,
The birds were flying under water,
The plants were spreading their sails,
I was taking root. The roots of the trees
Swung and swayed in the burnishing breeze.
But I heard above and beyond the leas
The wet sound of the water,
The dry sound of the palm.

Does the wind have a sound of its own?

                                    We know
The words of the wind, the truth of the trees,
The questions of water, the answers
Uttered by the shore—the shore
Of Troy, of Lesbos, of Athens, of sandy
Pylos, of Ithaca. We know how to sing
These answers. Don't smear wax
On your ears. Don't tighten the bonds
That restrain you. Don't refuse
To listen. Don't be afraid to come.

Does the wind have a sound of its own or only
The cluck of the water, the clack of the palm?

A creek flowed into the bay.

Across the creek
The four white egrets
Did their thing.
Two sat in trees:
One hunched asleep,
The other preened.
Two walked the shore:
One stalked the slope,
The other, wetting
Big black boots
In wading kept
His white parts dry.

Along the creek browsed Australian pines,
Birch-bark cajeputs, and gray-plated
Earleaf acacias. The acacia flowers
Are golden caterpillars and their fruits
Bronze labyrinths where, on sharp orange hooks,
Black beads hang gleaming.
I put one labyrinth into my handbag
And crossed the gray concrete bridge.

Whether the egrets were men
I wasn't quite sure, but the pigs were.
The women, though, said Circe, I turn
Into schoolgirls, to whom I teach skills
They need in a pig-run world. But you,
Since something has shown you the labyrinth (for
When she waved the pointer I, long-schooled, did not shrink)—
You, too, will instruct them. The schoolroom was restless
Like a pen of navy-blue, white-collared calves,
With big bronze eyes turned outward. Groping
Along the bronze passages, I imparted the thread
Which I could hardly claim to descry:
How to fast, how to feast, how to speak, and how
To shut up. Around us we heard
The endless rooting and grunting.

An egret—a white cloud in his tree—
Suddenly started to scratch his ear.

When a red bird bloomed in the oleander
And a green bird flew shrieking down the creek
And a blue bird flashed up into the cajeput
And the egret's camel S stretched into an I,
Then Circe said: It's time for you to go.
The waterlight spun on the white barber poles
As I pushed off against the current.

Across
The pool
The four
White blos-
Soms swam.
Beside
The spar-
Kling wa-
Ter sat
Helen
In her ba-
Thing suit
With her cig-
Arette
In her tanned
Fingers.

Jack, too shy to hand them to her,
Had set the flowers afloat. Yes,
She was beautiful. Yes, she was
A worthy daughter of deep-browed Jupiter.
Yes, you would almost have to believe
What she was saying: And therefore the ERA
Will damage fragile balances erected
Through centuries by western civilization.
We defeated the Trojans, an Asiatic race,
And now, without fear from abroad,
If we maintain our defenses at home,
We can enjoy in peace our Hellenic blessings. Women—
I know, for I have sinned—are fitted by nature
For marriage and for religion. Let them make heaven
And take their husbands along. I must
Give up smoking. Extending her arm,
She stubbed out her cigarette. She stood up,
Stepped to the edge, tensed, waited poised,
And dived into the pool. The white
Blossoms bobbed about her in a frenzy.

My oars were gone, my boat was smashed,
But I crawled up onto the shore
At the foot of the long mild slope of the lawn.
After about an hour I limped up the grass
And hobbled along the straight gray drive
Lined by stone gray columns of royal palm.
I remember at the end two fruiting cycads
And two date palms on their rooty hills
And the heavy door being pushed open.

I awoke in a sunny bedroom, watching
The sun in the thick green figleaves,
The sun in the long green fingers,
The sun in the long gold fingers,
Of queen palms, the sun in pink lips
Puckered around red tongues
Of triple-flowered hibiscus, the sun
In the screens, in the slats, on the sheet,
On her gray silk blouse. She looked anxious, then relieved.

Except for the three brawny maids who spoke
A language of unfamiliar intonation and refused
To raise their eyes even to my chin,
She was the only person on that island,
I found as I explored
Among its breezes. Golden gleams
In the scarlet threads of the callistemon,

Skyflowers, coral vines, queen's wreaths, flame vines
Found me. When I was well
And ready to say goodby, she interrupted:
Though I'm called Calypso, I will not hide
My thoughts. She took my hand
And drew it slowly between soft breasts.
Stay here, she said, and touched the top button
Of her sleek silk blouse. The rosy-lipped,
Red-velvet-tongued hibiscuses
Nodded by the hot white wall.
But as soon as Mercury descended
In his hydroplane, she let me go.

The Phaeacians smiled. The sun
Slanted like sleet through the slats
Of the jalousie windows, along
The princess's flaxen hair. Remain
And teach good Greek to our daughter,
The queen invited. But if you can't,
Stay as long as you can. And if you must go,
We'll help you. Just give us your name and address.

My name is Flora Urania Baum. My home,
Which I seek, is Ithaca Island, on which stands
A mountain rich in trees and rainbow flowers
With summits rising far above the gray
Of rains and mists and clouds into the great
Blue binding of our black-cased world. I seek tall oaks
And polychromatic flowerets—gold crepe, crimson
Silk, peach satin, velvet prussian blue,
And lace of burnt sienna. I must read,
Then, the candid letters on the spine.

Stay as long as you can. But if you must go,
We'll send you in our silver Cadillac.

                                        Smooth,
So smooth was that ride she awoke
Only at sunset near the bridge
Beyond the gray strait. What shall I say
Of the plow deep in the black earth,
Of the peak white against the sky?
The sky bound her. In the clarity of that night
She knew its blackness and the whiteness of each star.
Violet-sweet through the dark flew the scent of each butterfly flower.
And out past the palm tree's castanets
The sun rose over the cove's cloud-marbled floor.

3. Delphi

It has been asked before:
Why would anyone's tears
Greet the golden columns and the rosy cliffs?

He was a Greek god.
Do you understand? He was a god.
He stood there in his divinity.

I know about gods. They're not all the same.
Some—but why enumerate?
He—how shall I explain?

It was on the first day of April
That I left the shore and the port and began
My walk up the stream. The peaks rose beyond.

He should be back. It's spring.
Though the narcissus is hard,
The hyacinth tightly bound,

Squills in bluest profusion
Have poured into the channels of twilight,
Deep with copiousness.

Open your eyes. Though no groves
Of olive shimmer silver, though
No laurel waits in perpetual green,

Aspens strung with gray and red,
Alders strung with bronze and gold,
Stand without impatience.

And though no gleaming swan
Oars him stately along,
Seven wingèd swimmers play.

See duck. See duck.
Be our beggars.
Run for our crusts.

The ducks are so amusing,
Being ducks, ducking,
Tipping up those curly tails.

The ducks are so loquacious,
Uttering their respective syllables:
Their long spondees, their tribrachs and tetrabrachs.

The ducks are civilized.
Observe, after her invitation and his acceptance,
The courtliness of their mutual bows.

A duck has his pride.
There goes aggressive Achilles,
Rebuffed, striding down the lawn, sailing from the dissatisfactions of Troy.

Far above us ducks
Strain with the strength of pinions
As they peer through the miles.

She laughed. I enjoy them, too.
Did you see how the big white one
Sailed down the stream like a clipper ship,

Fought, and, waked by victory, returned?
I suppose, I said, he's the ugly duck
Among the mallards. If not quite a swan,

Though big, he's not domestic,
Feral at least, ferocious at times,
Off on his high charger to the attack.

I resent, though, his bellicosity, his
Womanizing. Nature, she said.
The race must go on.

Her gray eyes sparkled, her armor shone.
Am I not my father's child?
Her eyes, like olive groves, glimmered.

And so I went on up.
Summits attract. What can you do
But climb? Your spirit flutters

Almost with wings. You will see
Where you were and where you were not,
Where you are and where you are not,

Where you could be. You will choose
Among the visions, among the beauties,
Among accessible things,

Among inaccessible things—
The hyacinth and the farthest hill,
The odoriferous blue, the remote

Smoky blue. The old green of pines
Guarded the young green of the birches.
The young fluid green was smeared

Across the fabric, mixed with sun
Dipped from the tulips' unemptying cups.
A pretty picture? The cups

Filled and refilled, red, yellow, mauve,
Red jewel, yellow lantern, mauve
(Deep dark mauve) solar spring.

I drank. A pretty picture?
There he stood. Was it frightening?
Behind him rose the columns and the rocks.

A Greek god is a statue,
Naked, powerful, and perfect,
Every muscle of his marble arm

In harmony. Cold ancient youth,
What have you to do with me perusing
Your body—that buttock, that knee,

That perfect accusing or caressing arm?
I accept that accusation and that caress,
I am forced to accept, I am forced

To feel sun reach through cloud,
Blaming the disaffection of the eye,
Claiming the flesh that glowed

When beyond the frame, beyond the panes,
The box elder burst into lambent green flames
And shuddered its way to gold.

A Greek god is an actor
In an old play. He stands on the roof
And speaks iambic. A girl

Runs across the circle, tearing
The wreath from her unleashed hair.
Cruel! To make me tell yet tell in vain!

A sobbing woman pulls
Her cloak yet tighter, shaking.
Cruel! When I did yield to kill the child!

(Hedged about by lilac, on the youthful grass,
Things soft and fierce,
The green glittering sundrops of the birch beyond.)

From the roof the mask delivers
Deep-voiced the measured reply.
Your son lives on. Your words live on. You die.

This does not die: the bubble and swirl of robin song in the dusk,
The tune of slim birch gleam in April dusk, the purple notes
That spurt from the soil where the unearthly

Hyacinth sits on the earth and sings
Deep full gathered multitudinous song
Ascending April nightfall.

A Greek god is a breath
That carries an echo of music
Breathed on your ear, on your mouth, you can't breathe,

You can't hear, you hear that music, you breathe
That echo, it rattles in your chest, your chest
Echoes, you know you can't breathe, there's something

On your lips, on your tongue. At dawn,
In the silences between the intonations,
Half awake, half asleep, you repeat,

As though you heard a language recorded,
With silences between the uttered phrases,
The phrases of the thrush from the wood above the gully.

Listening. Singing. Wait.
Singing. Nothing other. Singing.
Listening. Wait. Singing.

Come on into the wood, she said,
If that's your notion of divinity.
I'll show you the way. There were no paths.

That she could slip through keyholes
I knew as I tried to follow,
Bending under branches, barging

Through brambles, sliding along
The moss, into mud, running along
The verdant three-leaved ivy, among

The ardent triple-tongued mosquitoes. Were the birds
Leading or fleeing as they flitted just ahead,
Ever ahead in the shadows? Beyond

The velvet-padded zigzag fence,
The swimming hole's brocaded edge,
We came to the lyrical brook.

When born among the quivering trees
I did not weep but on the breeze
Began to sing.

I sang a philosophical song
Of earth and stars and right and wrong
And wondering.

I felt the soil, I watched the sky,
I entered roots, was entered by
Far-falling rain.

I plunged beneath the whirling world
And leapt with silver wings unfurled,
Hot to explain

All that I thought. I thought. I lay
Along the grass all summer day
Deep in the shade,

Deep in the sun, silent, then stirred.
He came. He thought. He sang. He heard.
He was afraid,

Envied my effort and my rest,
And kicked a stone upon my breast,
And changed my tune.

I sing, I speak, I think, he said,
But to my infants and my dead
Low you may croon.

From the stadium where the young men strip off their clothes
And run the long race to the west, then turn and return,
You can see the blue gulf

Blazing as Greek gulfs blaze, without strain, and the young
Men's effort seems effortless, too, so graceful are they,
Like the grace of blue flame.

If you climb in the other direction, toward the east,
Up the cliffs, you reach the chilly, dripping cave,
High on Parnassus yet sunk deep into the earth,

Where nymphs whisper and whistle and mortal women
Unbraid their long hair. From that rocky, watery cave
(Confer Pausanias) even a well-girt male

Must sweat to attain the top. It's a hard ascent
And the peaks are above the clouds and upon the peaks
Thyiades rave

To the god with drums, with flutes, with chants, with cries,
With cries in their women's voices, with human cries,
Beauty will save,

And run down, down, down,
Dizzy, dizzy, down, down,
Spinning, tumbling, down, down,

Past the goats, the springs, down,
Past the firs, the cave, down,
Past the theater, down, down,

By the temple rising tall,
By the high retaining wall,
By the statues that will fall,

By the pillared stoa fair,
By the treasure houses rare,
By the ruins lying there,

Past the angry Centaurs, down,
Past the three-man Geryon,
Past the fighting giants, on

Past the warring heroes, on
Past the battling Amazon,
Past the goddesses and ducks, down, down.

Out by Twelvemile Brook
Where blackbirds flash red wings
Sped Artemis.

Over the Messalonskee
Where flickers glitter toward the bridge
Strode Athena.

On toward Mayflower Hill
With the blue glint of the swallow
Strolled Apollo.

4. Eleusis

She's gone. The earth is white. The sky
Is black. Footprints on the snow
Tramp into shadow.

     Did you think
When the leaves fell you would see
A gowned figure among the boles,
When the snow fell you would find
The light tracks across the plain,
When the night fell you would know
Her cry in the silence?

    All day
The chickadees called cold. Did you wait
Till the wind fell to ascend
The bitter hill? Did you turn
As you climbed to let the sun
Just for a moment feel your cheeks?
When the rain fell did you want
Ice to clench the earth? Did you say
No to the landscape? Did you say
No to the land?

     You must have clamped
Each hand around itself and pounded
Your chest, pressed your forehead, and knuckled
The cold sting of your tears. You stamped,
You ran against numbness into pain.
Your pain was a shout, a torch, a hound.
Was there a rush into your arms,
An answering "Mother, Mother"?

As you crossed the bridge you knew
Only your shadow was moving
On the white silence of the stream.

As you crossed the bridge you experienced
The gephyrism of the wind
Jeering. You hammered your ears.

As you crossed the bridge you bowed before
Vociferous sleet, mute swanlike winging snow.
The whishing, chugging motors of your feet
Driven down the dazzling lane
Reached the sonant fountains of the snowblowers
And dragged you to witness the agriculture of winter.
The snow is plowed and the frost blossoms.

                                        But where is she?

Behind the flower stood
Death.

          How in a moment
Transitions are made—how the green and golden
Universe instantaneously dissolves
With the brief misplacement of a foot,
With a slight papery slice across an eye,
With a willed or unwilled word—needs no explanation.
We all live at the edge. But one
So young, so lovely, so immortal—
How could she surmise
In the plucking of a single bloom
As her small hand drew away the flower
That brute plucking? The sod cracked.
He leapt upon her.

                    She lives now
In a lifeless region, under the sown seed.

And why did her powerful father look the other way?
To men is granted power, to women
The bearing of power. Earth
Bore Sky; to mighty Sky,
Her child, she bore strong sons
Whom he hated and hid. But his son
Unmanned his father, wedded
The wife who bore strong sons
Whom he hated and hid. But his son . . .

How did it end? To Death
He gave his daughter. He let her
Be hidden in Earth. Somehow it worked.
His sons were clones, skylings

(The mother merely bears the father's
Seed, averred the Athenian justice,
And she a goddess), his daughter
Rose with spring, descended
With every fall.

              That went on a long time.

Now it's March in Maine. There's summer in the sun.
Between us and summer, between us and the sun
Extends a chilly atmosphere. Yet noon
Reaches through, exciting sweetness
In the pallid grass.

              And something new,
More than the dead duck floating down the stream,
Emerges as the green ice breaks.

              We've tried—
Learning what happened when you picked that narcissus—
We've tried very hard to find you, goddess,
Girl, last seen running through a field
All bloom. We pondered in the syllables of the wind
Consonants, vowels, or only vowels,
Yes or no or only eh
Or oh. We got the message, we read
The fable, winter. We held up pines
As torches, saying, See, they're green,
There's green. The snow quenched that. That white
Refutation undid our names. We crawled
Through blackest caverns, hoping that here,
Far from the snow-glare, deep in the dark,
Freed from trying to see, free
To feel, we would touch your skirt.

              From the earth,
As the yellow tips turn green,
And the green-enfolded pillars build,
And the green wraps hint of gold,
As the snowdrops rise and the snowdrops fall,
And the slush, of rose and silver,
Fades into the watery twilight, and in the dusk
The white duck is a moon
Moving down the stream, and through
The bearable night the stream goes flowing,
And as at dawn the gold and white and green
Plunge below the bank, pointing to the blue
Center of the globe, like torches pointing,
And are not reflections, in that clarity
Are true trees, willow, birch, and pine,

Among green blades the white and golden
Maiden issues with a tune in her throat,
Rises with a pen in her hand,
Singing her own song,
Writing her own account.

Between sterility and stability,
Between continuation and dissolution,
Between life and life, and death and death,
The crocuses come, the roses come,
The leaves redden, the boughs grow white,
The crocuses come. They are not the same.
Spring is back, they say, you say.
Spring is not back. Spring goes forever.

Oh, our lovely Persephone has returned.
Am I the same, when I have seen
(Down there, where I sit in brocade,
With a scepter in my lace-gloved hand)

Achilles weep, Agamemnon warn
Against all women, Odysseus at last
(Ulysses no longer) close his eyes
To questing, Penelope set her hand
At best to her shuttling, and the web
Of the universe wax and decay?

Pericles came by, Napoleon
Shuffled over, Hitler dropped in
Heavily, and in a corner
Sappho sat at her lyre.
There grew an eternal garden
With everlasting tumbling runnels
And apple blossoms fresh forever
And rest rustling from the leaves.

Who wants apples when the apple blossoms
Are fresh forever? We want bread
But we want roses and the rose
That does not die.
                    Tithonus
Begged his end, and Sibyl prayed
Nine hundred years for instant death.

I have dropped my scepter, taken my pen,
And written what I saw as I ascended:
The splendid pallor of the grass,
The faint purple light of the crocus on the snow,
The dawn-orange song
Of the dawn-orange finch
In the dawn-orange elm.

There were many Caesars; there was one
Sappho with her lyre in her fingers,
Sappho with her pen in her fingers.

The willow strings of gold
Are gold against a sky of lead,
A gray-haired sky as oppressive as my father
Zeus. The strings shine gold against a sky
Of lapis lazuli. Where is the sky
Most blue? Where is the most acute
Blue, blue note of the curving lyre?
Why should the sky curve in upon us, pressing
Us back as our song expands, ascends,
Peers down?

                 Factories stand in the field.
Machines are busy making bread.
I am hungry. I reach out my hand.
How can you hear me above the machines?
I sing, I write, I cry.
Can you follow my tune,
Can you recognize my hand,
Can you hear me, Mother?
The alders gleam with bronze and gold.
As yet no narcissus is in flower.

5. Helicon

The Eleusinian solution,
A twofold proposal—
For the individual, personal life after personal death,
For the community, impersonal rhythms of impersonal ever-reliving
Nature, both now in doubt,
The one through progressive enfeeblement in the gods,
The other (this diagnosis is only too well known) through man's
Mad magical stretching of his long potent-impotent arms—
Did not of necessity directly affect
Artists qua artists, who went on adoring
Beauty or fame or excitement or joy
Or some other madness of their own.

And if
Beauty has faded with the gods
And must no longer be invoked
Or even named (if merely a mouthing
Of the appellation makes us blush), and fame
Will have nothing more to reflect it—no long
Capitol steps, bright dome, clear pool—
Will have nothing more to outlast—no statue,

No pyramid, no aquilonian wind—and pure
Joy apprehends the shadows
Of gaunt arms like bare branches
Clutching and crashing across
The continents, shall singing stop

Or shall some squatters under the mountain
Practice their tunes in the dark
Just in case a dawn
Should crawl their way, in case
Some listener with hungry ears
Should stumble toward them in that new morning?

Over there, in a corner behind
The black-and-white Baptist steeple
And the low brick gable of the public library,
There through Andrew Carnegie's disinterested generosity,
Rising an orange sun.
Trying to hold open for a moment and another
Sleep-closed, light-delighted eyes.

They were dancing around the violet spring
And around the smoking outdoor altar
Of mighty Zeus, high on the mountain.
The sheep all stopped, and the shepherd, climbing,
Climbed faster to see what could... He stopped,
He stepped back. Just barefoot girls,
Dancing in silence around the spring,
Nine, it seemed; but like no girls
Of Ascra or any village or farm
Or town that he knew. They were lithe and tall,
Their long curls glistened, their faces gleamed,
And their violet eyes, when the turns of the dance
Brought each before him, knew him through
And through. And then they began to sing.
No thrush at dawn, no nightingale at dusk,
No flute, no lyre, no selected choir
Would match or mimic those sounds—each voice,
Each note, each chord, each phrase, each tune,
Perfect, and the whole, perfection. His ears
Throbbed, his eyes were glazing, he could scarcely
Stand, he could hardly breathe. And then
They began to speak. They spoke to him.
Shepherd, they said, calmly, softly,
Shameful wild thing, belly only,
Dipping like a duck for bread, we can
Always express fiction as fact,
And we can when we want to tell what is true.

Each voice, though soft, though calm, echoed
In his ears. The soft grass yielded to their feet,
The soft, sweet air of morning caught,
Carried, passed along their song.
They danced beyond the columbines,
Beyond pale peach and palest purple
Irises edging the clearing, beyond
The laurels, beyond tall firs, through green
And shadow and dark and flicker and back
And a branch bent low to a slim white quest
And they turned with the laurel toward where he still stood
And into his shaking hand they set
The singer's staff, and dancing around him
They breathed through his gaping mouth a voice.
Of Zeus our father now you will sing
And of us and our harmonies first and last.
And still the morning was violet and rose.

The oriole's aubade, raying
As bright as his orange self.

On another mountain
Zeus spoke to Mnemosyne. Come,
Memory, to me, to the calling
Sky. Remember
The azure above white Athens,
The jagged stars over Delphi's blackness,
Olympic mists in which the sky
Went down to caress invisible rocks
And raucous tunes of unseen sheep
And the rain-green grass and the rain-gray sea.
Remember the sky as solid,
Motionless, metallic. Remember
The sky of moving parts, the machine
In full operation, the ragged clouds
Like hares, the smoother clouds behind
Like tortoises, the leisured moon,
The wandering stars on their old grand tour,
And the fixed stars, stuck,
Unstuck, and stuck again
Without clogging the parade. I mix
My metaphors. The sky,
Like fire, like frost, transforms
Its tropes as one applies them, slapping
Ferns and palms and hills and stars
Around like paint. Remember
The pigmentation, blue, as cold
As frost, ablaze like flame,

Piling through the miles, dissolving
Into dust, resolving
Into measureless sky. Remember
Thunder above the splitting trees,
Lightning sizzling through the room, raindrops
Nestling in the lilacs, glistening
Like small cupped stars. Do not forget
The age of the light of the stars. We sat
Together on that star's earth when the light
Which touches our eyes now set forth, passed us,
Warmed us as we played on another mountain
Nine thousand years ago, in our first youth.
Come,
Memory, to me, the
Sky.

Zeus shook his thundrous locks. His eyes
Were flashing. Hailstones crashed
On dark-cracked sod. Mnemosyne
Went. And they were born—
Nine healthy daughters. Forget
All your cares—all cares—for a moment. The nine
Immortal sisters come singing. The sky
Turns an echoing blue.

A tête-à-tête with a turtle,
Admiring the bright orange trim
And the black glitter of those eyes in the sun.

Another time Zeus said,
Leto, my love, I'm sick
Of my nagging wife. Let's go off together.
His wife was the queen of the gods, but he
Was the king. They went off together.

The mother, heavy with twins,
Came to Athens: No. Went to Athos: No.
Went to Samos, Scyros, Imbros, Lemnos:
No. No, no, no. She came
To Delos, less than two square miles
Of stone set in the sea.
Delos, will you receive me
For the birth of my son? Goddess,
I am afraid, for they say that Apollo
Will be a haughty god. No place
Will be good enough for his birth. He will
Despise his hometown, stamp his godly
Foot, and I will find
Fish swimming above my mountain.

I promise, the goddess replied,
This place shall be sacred to my son.
His temple will rise here and pilgrims
Come with rich gifts and rich hymns. If you promise,
Delos said, it shall be.

For nine days
Beside the palm tree on the slope of the mountain
She suffered, and on the tenth (you know how it went)
The precocious daughter, born first, assisted
Her mother to bring forth a son. He stood up,
Brushed back his flaxen curls,
Slung on his silver bow,
Took up his gold-keyed lyre,
Thought, and sang—the very lord
Of song.

How shall I hymn you,
All ways well-hymned Apollo?

Shall I watch you descend from the peaks of Olympus,
Your arrows clanging on angry shoulders,
Your coming like night? Shall I watch you sit
On a dune by the sea, and hear the twang
Of your silver bow, and see the mules
Die first, and then the dogs, and then
The heroes? Shall I hear
Cremating pyres, pyre upon pyre?

Shall I watch you ascend Olympus,
Easily climbing through the clouds,
And see the gods all tremble and stand
And your mother unstring your bow and cover
Your quiver and hang your bright weapons on golden
Pegs in your father's golden
Palace and Zeus in welcome
Hand you himself the golden
Cup brimming with golden
Nectar? And shall I watch
You reach for your lyre and pluck the golden
Strings and sing the golden
Songs and lead with high skilled step
The dance of the golden gods?

The papery poppies, orange, far
From sleep, all bright, all orange
Among the purples of the irises.

The first declension: femina, feminae; puella, puellae.
Feminae amicae sunt.

The second declension: vir, viri; puer, pueri.
Viri amici sunt.

The third declension: pater, patris; mater, matris;
Homo, hominis; omnis, omnis; aequalis, aequalis.
Omnes homines aequales sunt.

Once upon a time there was only
The third declension. Mais l'homme,
Hombre, uomo... What ever happened
To the good old virile term?
Why on earth was that inhumed?
Man became man. The other?
La belle et la bête.
From man to minx.

Words. Just words, whether just
Or unjust. Let us not fall into a
Decline. Let us arise.
Homo sapiens speaks
No Latin now, for he

Or she or even she or he may speak
A language of minimal inflection

And the aviatrix and the narratrix and the inheritrix
And the actress and the goddess and the heiress
And the authoress and the giantess and the princess
And the stewardess and the murderess and the poetess
Have or will have cut out their tricks
And cut their tresses
And dropped their s's.

How hard it would be
If we spoke Greek.

Le roi est mort. Vive la reine.
Le le est mort. Vive la la.
Over here luckily we have
No royalty, few divinities,
Room for creators and creatrices,
For we hold these truths.

The bride and the bridegroom walk up the aisle.
The man and the wifeman walk down the street.

And life goes along
As the stream beneath monoecious and dioecious trees
And the ducks and the drakes on top of the stream
And the monkeys and apes on top of the trees,
And with much travail the masterpiece is made
And after long labor the mastersinger sings
His song. She sings a mistresssong.

Gazing deep into the deep
Purple of the iris, glinting
Sharp in high noon, soft, deep.

Color into which you gaze—
Not into the iris—into the sheer
Depths of purple, into those depths.

Purple petals lifted,
Purple petals open-armed,
Purple tuneful tongues.

At dusk a purple dark to black.
Behind, rising, white
To purple, whitest purplest white.

Three threes seen,
Dark, centered, deep,
Three purple threes.

Behind the dark the light,
Before the light the dark,
White to purple, purple to black.

One in three threes,
One darkest flower,
Three threes in one.

Flexible, changing, soft,
Strong, unchanged, unconquerable,
Let us say, given the winters.

A dark look, prolonged
In longing, into the heart
Of deep green and purple June.

Father Zeus. Father O'Flaherty.
Father il Papa. Pater noster.
Father George Washington. Uncle Sam.
Uncle Hades. Father Freud.
Pater omnipotens Deus. By Jupiter,

Once there was a father who spun.
He couldn't fix the faucet or a broken doll,
He couldn't drive an auto or a needed nail,
But he could spin. Tell us a story.
You're here. Tell us a story.

I have to get wound up, he would say,
And somehow his daughters devised a plan
Of twisting their fists near his head or his arm.
On the evening of which I speak, he would say,
And then they would not move. Their eyes,
Big, round, almost unblinking, were fixed
Upon the ever-moving thread.

On the evening of which I speak,
Annabel and Isabel were sitting
In the great green chair.

                        From a place like that
Adventure drew through Chew-Gum Forest,
By Lolly-Pop Copse, up Sun-Up Hill,
Where the chugging bus would pass you full
Of all the girls and boys you'd know
In years to come: Elizabeth and John,
Samuel and Virginia, Celeste and Antoine—
This one tall, black-haired, black-eyed,
With a bright green collar; that one, short,
With auburn curls and a pale blue belt.

Patrick and Pericles, the Mischief-Makers,
Would play some tricks, and the Tick-Tock Dogs
Throw motion pictures in your path to lead
Explorers astray.

                    But you'd find a friend,
Maybe Philip, though he was very small,
Having been made of the last of the dough
When the Pumpernickels were baked for the tree;
Or Peter, the first to reach up his hands,
Untie the red ribbon, and jump to the floor,
And announce from the middle of the old green rug,
In the middle of the room, in the middle of the building,
In the middle of Chicago, in the middle of America,

That he was Peter Pumpernickel
And had a cousin Lily Pickle
And was made of ginger bread;
He'd a ginger coat and a ginger vest
And he did his ginger, ginger best.

With Peter or Paul or Percival you'd reach—
After wondrous excitements along the way
(To make a short story long, he would say),
Past the Topsy-Turvy House (Which side
Was floor or ceiling, ceiling or floor?) —
The Golden Playground. There the swings
Could swing you anywhere: Denver; California,
Where the mountains come down to the edge of the ocean;
Peking; Moscow; Paris; London;
Bangor, Maine; or Austin, Texas;
Buenos Aires, Argentina;
Resolute; Komsomolets;
Cook Ice Shelf; Dibble Iceberg Tongue.

And then do you know what happened?
O no, O no, the children would cry.
They woke up, he said.

And went on to adventures of their own.
His grave, at his request, read, Penitent.

She must blame the fathers: Father Pacelli,
Father Zeus, and Father O'Malley,
Uncle Dis (polyonymous),
Uncle Sam (pseudonymous),
Founding Father (anonymous),
Jupiter (synonymous);
But that father of joy and adventure
She may not censure.

Irises' various purplings among
The opening strong
Orangenesses of the lilies.

The shepherdess was gathering flowers.
Girls will do that, you know.
Heidi, Europa, Creusa, Persephone,
Flora, all gape and gasp and gaze
After those bits of—what shall I say—
Of color, of odor, of texture, of form,
Those bits of beauty, they might say (poetesses),
Gazing at delphiniums growing toward the blues
Of meridians, gasping at the sunrise—
Orange, yellow, rose—of the snapdragons below them,
Gaping at the quintessential columbines
In fivefoldness, with their comet tails,
Or clematis lit purple on the lamppost,
Or catalpa blossoms bee-sweet on the tree.

She heard a noise among the leaves
By the stream. Black-masked for the ball
The cedar waxwing danced. And masks
Crossed other faces, or should she
Have gouged those pin-prick eye-holes
On her own persona? But her eyes
Were wide open. She looked
Before she leapt.

                    Was he a flower?
Or a songbird? Dulcet on the branches?
From which a melody or fragrance reached
Her senses, touched them, took them away?
From her to him? To hues before
Unseen, to notes unheard? Inside

A gray jacket? Under a tan leather
Vest? Under a loud authoritative
Hi? Did sunrise, melodious
In orange and rose, expand
And the snapdragon snap her up?
Was she gone?

        Was he a tree?
To climb as boys climb trees?
Grabbing, holding, hugging, victor?
One with those long arms, with large
Grasping, granting hands? Hands
On her hair, on her shoulders, on her, throbbing
With mighty pulsations, with spring's
New sap, with old
Old tunes?

        Was he a stream?
Filled with clouds and sky? Not the stream
Of February, when solely moving, slowly across the bridge,
Went lengths of train laden from the northern forests? Not the stream
Of reeds and trees rooted in ice? Not the stream
Of ice? A stream with the liquid scent
Of water flowing, the sunny scent
Of grasses growing on the bank, the scent
Of wild sea roses at the edge? A stream
Of the rippling rose of sunset,
The oriole's last flash to the nest
Dangling over the darkening mirror,
The robin's gurgle of goodnight,
The final completorial ripple of the thrush?
A splash—the last flick of a swallow,
Her white breast meeting the dim
Breast of the water, or was it the moon
In whiter nudity plunging?
And did she throw herself in?

The turtle turned, slid down the stony
Bank, slithered through tall grasses,
Went swimming muddily off. But when
I came back, the turtle was back, a bit upstream,
On the mown grass, taking the sun. I took care
Where I cast my shadow.

        Or was she accosted,
As one is in summer by fragrances,
By the nine immortal women singing?
Two or three would have been enough,
But nine all going at once

As when you saunter by the stream on an evening
And all the birds are going at once
With a rondo here, a mazurka there,
Here a sonata, there a waltz,
Or basil and garlic and dill,
And broccoli dewy and blue in the garden,
And pineapple woody and leaved on the table.

Hail, O Heliconiades, hail.
What shall I sing?

White, white, white,
The snow, the ash, the bride.

The businesswoman's elegant violet sandals,
The elegant elevation of those elegant slender heels,
Below the slender shapely shaven legs.

Brew, brew, brew,
The brew in the indigo bowls.

Her blue-striped shopping bag lying on the avenue,
The paper in it to be saved,
Not thrown with her into the Hudson River.

The green garland, not of bay—
Of thyme or parsley.

Goldilocks with her broom, sweeping,
Sweeping her way through the kitchen,
Sweeping into the empyrean.

Bathed and veiled, the widow stepping
Proudly into the orange blaze.

Blood, blood, blood,
Coming, coming, coming,
Her bloody red blood.

The sky tonight as echoing the Muses,
Or Muses ever echoing the sky.

The sun set to
The robin's darkening antiphon.

                          Oh,
They bathed in the limpid Permessus.
Their feet felt rocks and leaves and mud.
They bent down and splashed clear water
On smooth breasts and over smooth shoulders
With splashings like song. And no one saw them.

They walked beneath the great elm.
That wasn't hard to see

Between the Doric chapel
And the great Corinthian library.

Obscure Judiths were now permitted
Within the great university.

The elm, though American, not Ionic,
Combined Ionicity of line

And curve with its barbarous exuberance,
Standing there old and young, brown

And green, unmoving and moving,
Mother and maid in one,

Like the strong mother with rough strong hands
That rubbed your blouses on the washboard
And wonderfully rubbed your bed-hot back
And wonderfully summoned strong tones or soft
From the old piano; the same strong mother
With the soft girl's voice that sang
The morning songs, that read
The bedtime stories, the bedtime poems
Whose echoes never ended. You hear them.

The tree in the breeze is a stream or an ocean.
Then are the sparrows sandpipers,
The sociable pigeons seagulls,
These hot stone chapel steps the sand?
One could swim in the waves of the leaves
Or along the current of the trunk.
The leaves look cool like clear green waters.
The ridged brown current looks strong.
It would carry you swiftly away.
It carries you swiftly away
Along its irresistible lines,
Along its total air-bordered form,
Upward, upward, outward, outward,
Away. Where? You're almost there.
Dust blows. A city stands on this shore.
And the leaves? If you dive into the leaves
They are waves and particles, going and remaining,
Waves of music not subject to time
All summer. Do you prefer
This then to a genuine ocean—
An ocean tossing its leaves
Like a great blue tree?
                    From below,
In the shade of the afternoon current,
Under the sun-soaked waves,
You find cool green light coming through.

You find not merely form,
Not merely pure form of desire,
But useful things: oxygen, shade,
Ecstasy, strength, escape, relief.
                                   Oh,
They walked by the lingering Messalonskee.
She certainly saw them there.
The still brown stream was a long, long trunk.
At the little dam was a swish as of leaves.
Clear song rippled clear air.

Below stern pines and breezy willows
A moon crouched in the mud.
Above, in orange plenitude a moon
Stepped shimmering.

                    Walk with me, moon,
Beside neat blue luxuriance of spruces,
Beside wild silvery luxury of maples,
Beside smooth coppery lushness of the maples,
Beside amplitudinous greenery of this maple,
And stop by the steeple.
Bold, you remain in the open,
While I, half domestic, climb up the bank,
Obscured on the mud like a slumbering duck,
But I do not sleep, I possess the moon,
She said, or its bright companionship,
Or am possessed. It dazzles now
And now transforms an island cloud
Into a habitable desert. And now
The clouds go, and the steeple and the tree
And the nighthawk, shouting, shooting, and the cat
And I and the moon possess the night.

Is possession equal to desire?
Form is that desire,
Felt and found and formed,
Informed, deformed, reformed, then
Felt and found and formed again,
Like frost, like fire,
Like waters cooled and pavements warmed,
Like something almost possessed,
Restful and never at rest.